SILLY SIGNS

SILLY SIGNS

THE GOOD, THE BAD AND THE MAD

ARCTURUS

ARCTURUS

This edition published in 2013 by Arcturus Publishing Limited
26/27 Bickels Yard, 151–153 Bermondsey Street,
London SE1 3HA

ISBN: 978-1-78212-282-1
AD003652EN
Supplier 23, Date 0513, Print Run 2533
Printed in China

The sign outside the church proclaims, 'There are some questions that cannot be answered by Google.' By the same token, there are some jobs that cannot be done better by computer – and one of them is creating signs. The signwriter's art fulfils a multitude of purposes: to warn, to welcome, to alert, to reassure, to attract, to deter…Whether through words or pictures, a truly great sign tells us something about the person who created it – such as the image of a car that appears to have veered to the opposite side of the road just to run over a man, or the sign offering a wedding dress for sale: 'Worn once, by mistake'. Unfortunately, not all signs tell the story they were intended to tell, but that doesn't make them any less noticeable, or indeed entertaining. In fact, as this collection of silly signs proves, the accidental ones are often the best of all.

The more you look at it, the more it seems to tell a story.

Wouldn't it be quicker just to write 'toilet'?

Yeah, right.

At the Acme Boarding School for Boys, matron gets tough on personal hygiene.

No overtaking.

That's not the depth, it's the height you'll end up if you don't obey this notice!

Eventually, Maurice in signage was sacked for dithering.

Stop sniggering and watch the road!

It doesn't matter how clear you make your sign, THEY CAN'T READ!

The police here are leaving nothing to chance.

Ha! It's actually left.

The burghers of this alpine resort *really* want to hold on to their clientele.

And watch out for praked cras.

Todd began to regret smoking that funny cigarette on his break.

Well, what else do you call someone who's reached the top in the bait business?

But she's not bitter.

Don't tell teacher.

I'm asking you nicely. . .

Bulk discounts available.

Quite right. And don't trust your feet either!

ABSOLUTELY NO BOTTOM WASHING PERMITTED

We're watching you.

. . . but ask the wearer first.

Those penguins will do anything to cadge a ride out of here.

People entering the hospital were given a stark reminder
of the possible outcomes.

He came out today.

Anticipating a Vice Squad swoop, Big Vince alters the evening's billing.

On reflection, the owner of this hostel agreed he should have given a bit more thought to branding.

But brake too hard
And you may find
You in ditch
With car behind.

Just when you thought you'd found the perfect picnic spot.

Look what happens when you teach crocodiles to write.

Get round that!

An enterprising way to get rid of termites.

Thanks, but I'll use the stairs.

Children under 10 must be accompanied by a penguin.

So much worse than the gradual kind.

Once you've tried the food, you might feel this is the better option.

Alternatively, just go back to your car.

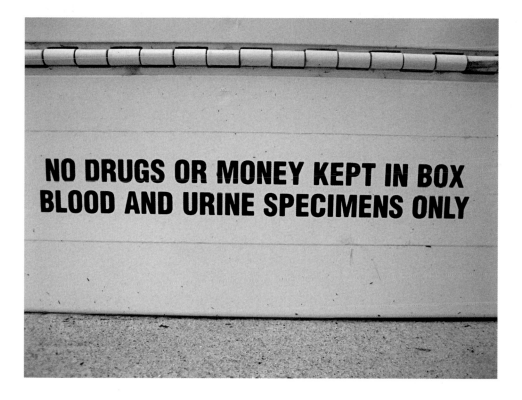

NO DRUGS OR MONEY KEPT IN BOX
BLOOD AND URINE SPECIMENS ONLY

Lance Armstrong's glovebox.

Aim high.

Not so macho now, are we?

Eric had never enjoyed such a prolonged spell of peace.

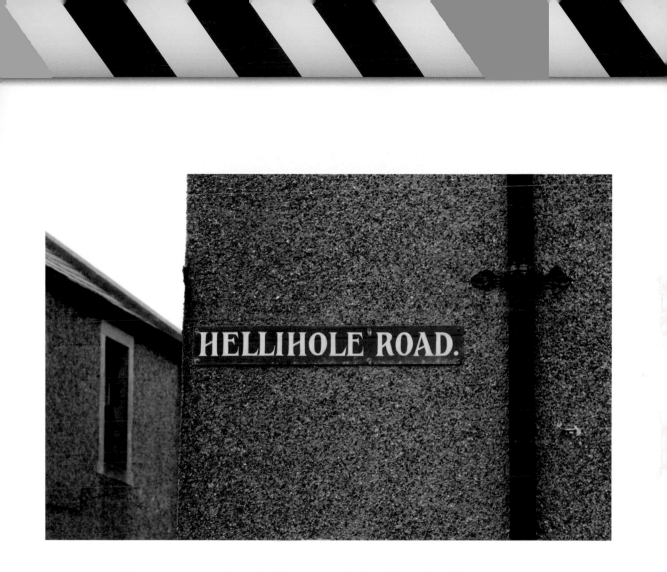

Between Snakeypit Street and the Slough of Despond?

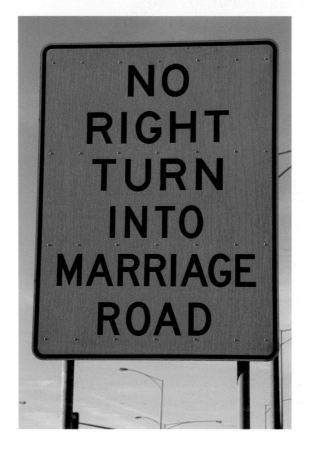

Not a great moment to propose.

You know it makes sense.

There's a shortage of eat-in toilets at present.

But this one almost fits the bill.

Red rag to a bull?

Wardens at the exotic tree farm fear the wurst.

You come all this way for black eggs . . .

Yes, but are the rooms clean?

It just smells that way.

Let's not go there!

こちらには ⛔ 押せません

再入園できません
CANNOT RE-COME IN

No second chances. If you don't come in properly the first time,
you don't get to try it again.

Now that's what I *call* consumer choice!

That's actually quite reassuring.

Flushing a sub-continent is a lousy job, but someone's got to do it.

I don't think they mean in the tow truck sense.

Heh heh heh!

Feeling lucky?

化粧室は後方へ
For Restrooms
Go back toward your behind.

It's a bit like following your nose.

Or you'll be s-s-sorry.

Give me that again...!!!??

Those with permission may trespass at will.

I get the feeling they mean it.

Towels not provided.

Alligator molesters were forced to go elsewhere for their fun.

Be honest, it's the last two words that catch your eye.

You can tell from that shifty-looking awning.

But smart drivers use a shotgun.

厕所 TOILET →

Wheelchair users please ring for assistance.

Huh, drains blocked again.

Raspberry works best, but apricot or blueberry will do.

Market traders challenge customers to a game of Articulate.

Who does this guy think he's kidding?

An existential thought-provoker to help pass the journey.

Hell, chuck it where you like!

Bet you wish you'd learnt Japanese.

Beware very long motorcyclists.

It's raining men!

Police boots shortage doesn't hamper war on crime.

They love visitors at No. 39.

The animal sanctuary's breeding programme just got too successful.

Quick – before he gets home from work!

We love pets, but we hate spelling.

Latest campaign to put the 'cool' in 'school'.

Not if you're trying to lift a fridge, it's not.

Beyond that, it appears, anything goes.

Never one to assume, Paddy the penguin checks the restrictions before joining his friends at the exclusive new rock club.

We only tolerate high-fliers in this neighbourhood.

I'll take a dozen, and a pound of duck cheese please.

The old jokes are the best.

Honey, can you remember where we left the car?

Welcome. If you can be bothered . . .

To be honest, it's been a constant problem since we took the warning sign down from the cliff.

NO RUNNING
OR HORSEPLAY
NO DOGS
NO NUDIES
NO BIKING
ROLLERBLADING
SKATEBOARDING

Granville Island

False Creek
Community Centre

Now go have FUN!

If you've reached ground level, you've gone too far.

C'mon, it's not difficult!

Everybody say 'whaay-oh!'

Yeah, make your mind up!

An unbleatable offer.

I think we get the message.

But if the cap fits, wear it.

The signwriter remembers the brief, a little too late.

You'll need one afterwards, though.

I get the feeling service is not going to be speedy!

5 MIN. WALK (IF RUN A LOT)

Ah yes, the old alligator-infested wheelchair trap. Always best avoided.

Now that's just mean!

I'm a rebel, me.

Wine and minglement – the very essence of Christmas!

The 11th commandment.

You see what they've done here?

. . . but where do you go for a blowout?

Welcome to the Retired Mime Artists Golf & Country Club.

Servicing all major airports.

Reserved for Arnie.

The marketing guys really went to town with this one.

Best not to argue.

返回里新购宗

VISIT IS OVER.
IF YOU WOULD LIKE TO RETURN,
YOU HAVE TO BUY TICKETS AGAIN

Now's the time to think long and hard – was it worth it?